Great Western
Broad Gauge Album

Compiled by A.K.Steele

Oxford Publishing Co

SBN 902888 11 0

Set by Oxford Typing Service Ltd., Oxford
Printed in the City of Oxford

Published by
Oxford Publishing Co.
5 Lewis Close
Risinghurst, Headington
Oxford.

PREFACE

The broad gauge died on the 20th May, 1892. None of us, apart from a very few octagenarians, have known it, and I have compiled this collection of photographs to give, I hope, an idea of what it was like. It is not meant as a historically representative cross-section of the period, but my personal selection depicting my favourite aspects of the scene.

I have deliberately intended not to do a 'whitewash' job and pretend that everything was sweetness and light; this was a new venture in the early days of railways, and things went wrong; men, even great ones made mistakes, and although I personally consider that broad gauge locomotives were generally the most successful of their time, nobody on this side of the Iron Curtain could say that they were generally the epitomy of grace and beauty—I did hear once that the sight of a Pearson 9 footer was the nearest thing to an instant hangover cure.

I have included a majority of photographs of locomotives, for they were the very life-blood of the railway, and the official side views, whilst not giving an impression of speed and power on the move, are far more interesting to the lover of the steam locomotive in detail than the blurred action shots which are the alternative. It is indeed unfortunate that photography was in its infancy at the zenith of the broad gauge, but in compensation we have the superb collection of the Rev. A. H. Malan taken in the eighties and nineties depicting the end of the era, and which I have included where appropriate.

Some of the pictures have been previously published, and I make no apology for including them in this collection as I feel that a repeat showing is warranted especially as they are of a larger format. The majority of the photographs are the property of British Railways, and are reproduced with their kind permission. Without their help this book could not have been produced and I express my sincere and grateful thanks for the assistance which I have received from Mr. N. Sprinks, Mr. W. R. MacDonald, and last but not least Philip J. Kelley, who set the wheels in motion.

I have gleaned information from many sources too numerous to mention specifically, but in particular from the *History of the Great Western Railway* by E. T. MacDermot, and the indispensable R.C.T.S. publications *Locomotives of the Great Western Railway*. I make no claim of absolute accuracy, as information has in certain cases been vague or contradictory, and I can only hope that my deductions are correct.

Here then is *Broad Gauge Album*. If it raises a sigh of nostalgia for the expansive and pioneering days of Brunel and Gooch then I will have achieved my purpose—and someone, somewhere, may even be moved to capture the scene in a broad gauge model railway.

Keith Steele. April 1972

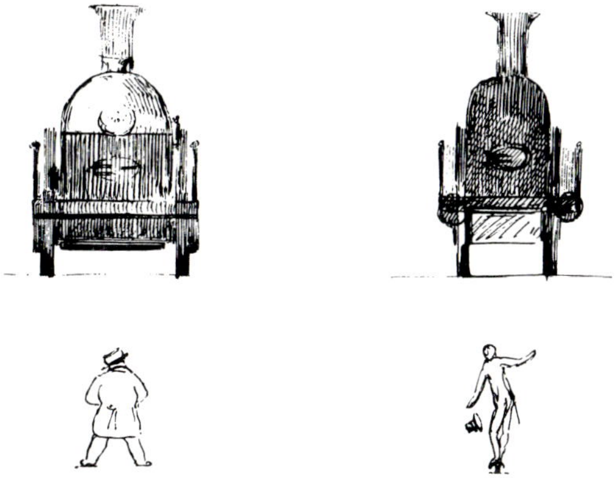

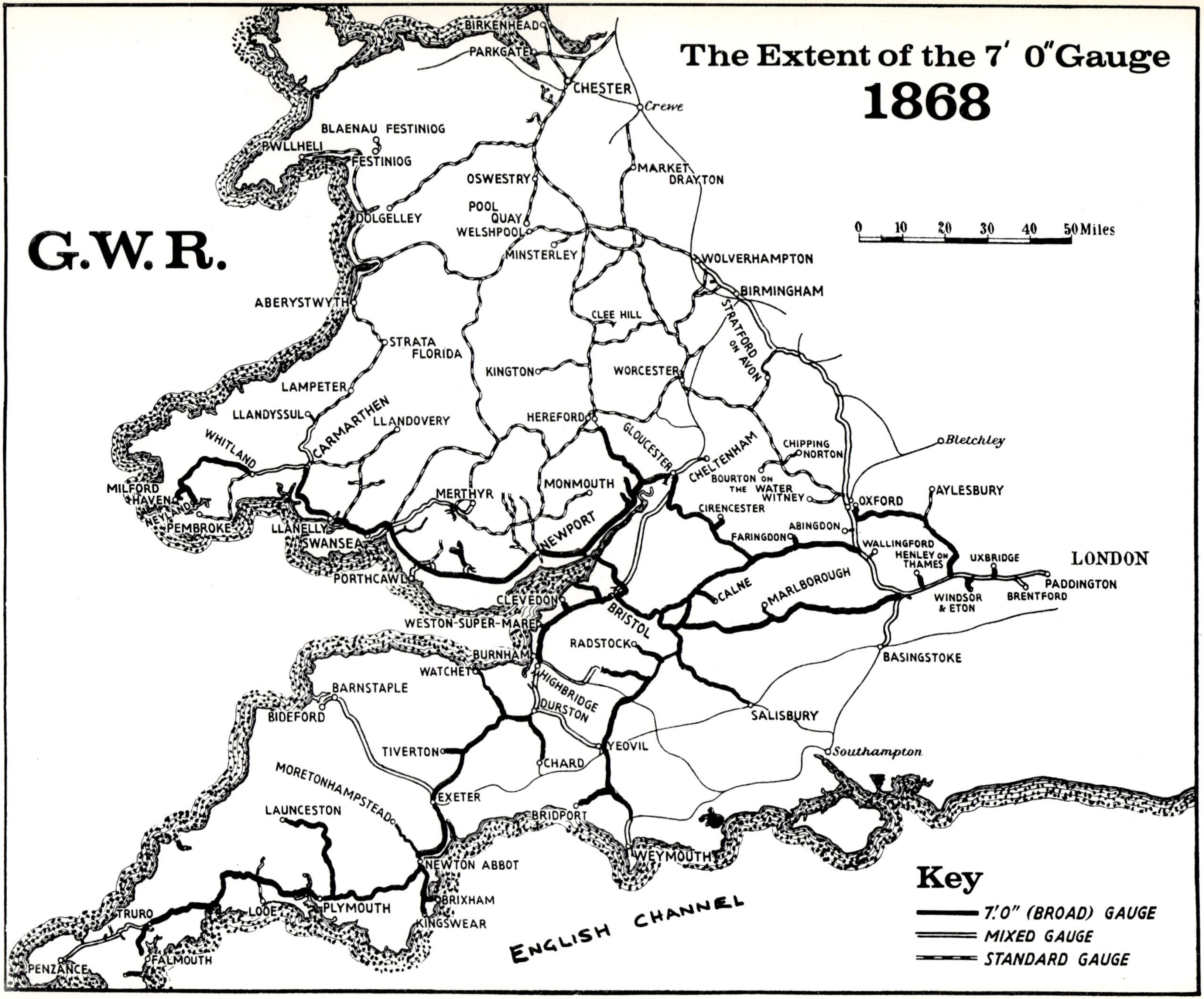

The Extent of the 7' 0" Gauge
1868
G.W.R.
BIRKENHEAD
PARKGATE
CHESTER
Crewe
BLAENAU FESTINIOG
PWLLHELI
FESTINIOG
MARKET DRAYTON
OSWESTRY
POOL QUAY
WELSHPOOL
DOLGELLEY
MINSTERLEY
WOLVERHAMPTON
BIRMINGHAM
ABERYSTWYTH
CLEE HILL
STRATFORD ON AVON
STRATA FLORIDA
KINGTON
WORCESTER
LAMPETER
CARMARTHEN
LLANDOVERY
LLANDYSSUL
HEREFORD
GLOUCESTER
WHITLAND
CHELTENHAM
CHIPPING NORTON
Bletchley
MILFORD HAVEN
NEYLAND
PEMBROKE
MERTHYR
MONMOUTH
BOURTON ON THE WATER
WITNEY
OXFORD
AYLESBURY
LLANELLY
SWANSEA
NEWPORT
CIRENCESTER
ABINGDON
FARINGDON
WALLINGFORD
HENLEY ON THAMES
UXBRIDGE
LONDON
PORTHCAWL
CALNE
MARLBOROUGH
PADDINGTON
CLEVEDON
WINDSOR & ETON
BRENTFORD
WESTON-SUPER-MARE
BRISTOL
RADSTOCK
BASINGSTOKE
BURNHAM
WATCHET
HIGHBRIDGE
DURSTON
BARNSTAPLE
BIDEFORD
SALISBURY
TIVERTON
YEOVIL
CHARD
Southampton
MORETONHAMPSTEAD
EXETER
LAUNCESTON
BRIDPORT
WEYMOUTH
NEWTON ABBOT
BRIXHAM
KINGSWEAR
PLYMOUTH
LOOE
TRURO
FALMOUTH
PENZANCE
ENGLISH CHANNEL
0 10 20 30 40 50 Miles
Key
7'0" (BROAD) GAUGE
MIXED GAUGE
STANDARD GAUGE

INTRODUCTION

The Broad Gauge was different. To its protagonists it was farsighted, revolutionary, and the model for future railway development; to its antagonists it was unconventional, reversionary, and an obstruction to through communication; but all would agree, it was different, and nothing like it has existed before or since.

It was conceived by Isambard Kingdom Brunel during his survey of the course of the line between London and Bristol in 1833 and 1834. As he set out the characteristic Brunelian wide radius curves and minimal gradients, he pondered on the suitability of the so-called 'Coal Waggon' gauge of 4'8½", thus far adopted by the other pioneer railways. In his own words '. . . *it seemed to me that the whole machine was too small for the work to be done, and that it required that the parts should be on a scale more commensurate with the mass and the velocity to be attained*'. So, the gauge was to be broad, but how broad? In his report to the directors in September 1835 he suggested that the carriage bodies should be contained within the wheels and proposed a gauge of 6'10" to 7'0" to '. . . *admit of sufficient width of carriages for all purposes*'. Thus, with the addition of a quarter of an inch for luck, the broad gauge of 7'0¼" was born.

And what a child it was. Brunel, not content with an unorthodox gauge, designed the track with longitudinal instead of cross sleepers, tied to the formation with piles. He also produced unworkable specifications for the locomotives. The track, after early modifications including dispensing with the piles, proved to give an exceptionally smooth ride although, according to some drivers, it did not have the 'give' associated with conventional track. The original locomotives, however, were an absurd collection of freaks built by various builders in an attempt to comply with the impossible specifications and, with few exceptions, did no useful work on the line. The only bright star in Brunel's firmament, if I may be permitted the pun, was *North Star*. A 5'6" gauge 2–2–2 which had been left on the hands of the builders, Robert Stephenson & Company, and which, with her sister *Morning Star* was converted to the 7'0¼" gauge. These engines formed the basis of Gooch's further designs culminating in the 8 foot singles for which the broad gauge is best remembered.

With Gooch now firmly in the saddle, a breed of locomotives appeared unlike anything else running on a British railway. With their domeless boilers and, on most classes, fully exposed wheels, they definitely looked different, but their performance belied their appearance, and with their help the broad gauge attained a reputation which was second to none.

Unfortunately, the broad gauge was laid just a few years too late to be anything but the odd man out, and the subsequent transshipment problems, aggravated by the non-co-operative policy of the narrow gauge companies, led in 1845 to the issue of a Royal Commission to investigate the advisability of a universally standard gauge for the railways of Great Britain. The 'Gauge Commission', as it became known, after hearing much evidence and conducting experiments at Brunel's suggestion to test the performance of broad and narrow gauge engines with similar trains, reported the following '. . . *whilst we feel it a duty to observe here that the public are mainly indebted for the present rate of speed and the increased accommodation of the railway carriages to the genius of Mr Brunel and the liberality of the Great Western Railway Company* . . .', '. . . *[we] consider a break of gauge to be a very serious evil*' and '. . . *the gauge of 4 feet 8½ inches be declared . . . to be the gauge to be used in all public railways now under construction or hereafter to be constructed in Great Britain*'. Thus they regretfully, it seems, set the seal on the death sentence of the broad gauge.

After wordy protests from the Great Western faction, permission was granted for proposed branches and connecting lines within the G.W.R. network to be constructed to the broad gauge, but the end result was still inevitable. In 1866, when the broad gauge was at its zenith, consisting of 600 route miles with 230 miles of mixed gauge out of a total of 1250 miles, Daniel Gooch broached the subject of conversion to a general meeting, and it was agreed that conversion should commence as soon as funds would allow. The programme was started in 1869, with the Hereford and Gloucester line and associated branches, continuing with the South Wales line and branches in 1872. Various other piecemeal conversions were made, until by December 1875 nearly 700 miles of track had been dealt with and only 8 miles of purely broad track remained (with about 120 miles of mixed gauge). However, in 1876 the Bristol and Exeter, South Devon, Cornwall, and West Cornwall railways were incorporated into the Great Western, adding a further 400 miles or so of broad or mixed track. Various branch conversions were carried out in the 1880s, culminating in the final conversion of the remaining 177 route miles of broad and 252 route miles of mixed track (mostly in Devon and Cornwall) which was carried out over the weekend of May 20th to 23rd, 1892. This massive operation was carried out with the aid of 4,200 men drawn from all over the system and, apart from preliminary work and later tidying up, was carried out on the Saturday and Sunday; the full passenger service recommencing on Monday, May 23rd.

The broad gauge at its zenith was considerably superior to its contemporaries in terms of speed, weight hauling and smooth running, but with the abolition decision came a reluctance to improve or develop new stock. No new designs of locomotives were built, apart from the convertibles, in the very last years, but these were standard gauge designs temporarily fitted with broad gauge wheels. Even the renewals of Gooch's famous 8 foot singles were built to the original details, apart from a small increase in boiler pressure. New coaching stock was built to standard gauge dimensions and fitted with broad gauge bogies and thus gained nothing in accommodation from the wider gauge. One must accept that this policy was perhaps justified on economic grounds, but one cannot help pondering on the outcome had the broad gauge been developed in line with, or to the exclusion of, the standard into the twentieth century. The sight of a broad gauge *Great Bear* or *Saint* would have surely convinced even the most diehard antagonists that this really was the GREAT Western Railway.

Problems arising from the break of gauge at Gloucester.

Vulcan. Built in 1837 with 8′0″ driving wheels by Charles Tayleur and Company of Newton-le-Willows. She was the first engine to work on the G.W.R., on the 28th December 1837 when she ran from West Drayton to Langley. She was one of the few early workable engines and ran in her original state until 1843 when she was rebuilt as a 'back tank' (shown in this photograph). *Vulcan* ran in this condition until April 1868 when she was put into use as a stationary boiler at Reading, being finally withdrawn in July 1870.

This view of the reconstruction of the opening of the line to Maidenhead staged in 1935 was in connection with the Centenary Celebrations held in that year. It shows the replica of *North Star* in her original condition, which was built in 1925 for exhibition at the Stockton and Darlington Centenary. This engine is now preserved in Swindon Museum.

Although the *North Star* as built, was, with her sister, *Morning Star*, the most useful engine on the line, there was still room for improvement. In 1854 she was rebuilt with a domeless boiler and front end refinements. Finally withdrawn from service in 1871 and stored at Swindon until 1906 when she was scrapped.

Firefly, with 7'0" wheels was the first of a class of 62 engines built between March 1840 and December 1842 to Gooch's first design by seven different manufacturers, *Firefly* being built by Jones, Turner and Evans of Newton-le-Willows. They were most successful engines and handled the bulk of the passenger traffic until the advent of the 8 foot singles. *Firefly* is recorded as having taken a directors' train of three vehicles from Paddington to Reading in 45 minutes, a very creditable effort for such a small machine, and she achieved 58 miles per hour on the return journey. *Ixion*, a member of the 'Firefly' class, was chosen to represent the Great Western at the Gauge Commission Trials in 1845 and soundly trounced the opposition. By 1865 they were outclassed for main line express work and were all withdrawn between that date and 1878.

Argus shows detail differences, being built in 1842 by Fenton, Murray and Jackson of Leeds to the same specification. She was rebuilt in 1864 with a raised round top firebox and longer boiler, making her similar in appearance to *North Star*. She was finally withdrawn from service in 1873 and sold for further work at the Bristol Colliery Company.

Sylph was one of the 'Prince' class of 2–2–2s with 7'0" driving wheels built in 1846. This was the first complete class of engines to be built at Swindon. They were intended as a lighter alternative to the 'Great Western', which had been outshopped earlier that year. They had inside frames only, making a saving of between 2 and 3 tons in weight. Only ten were constructed and, after initial work on the main line, they were relegated to the Birmingham line, where they survived until 1870.

Sultan, one of the first batch of Gooch's famous '8 foot singles', the 'Iron Duke' class. Built in 1847 incorporating improvements made to the *Great Western*, including the now standard raised firebox and the addition of an extra pair of carrying wheels at the front. These wheels were not arranged as a bogie, but were rigid in the frames with limited sideplay in the axleboxes, the driving wheels being unflanged to allow additional movement on curves. The original design of the bellmouth chimney can be seen, also the lack of protection for the crew and sparse backplate. The drivers of these engines must have been really 'hardy'. Viewing the road ahead whilst travelling through rain at 50 m.p.h. would have required great endurance. This particular engine was used as a model by Frith for his famous painting of Paddington station. It was withdrawn from service in 1874.

Lord of the Isles. Surely the most famous of all Broad Gauge engines. One of the 'Courier' class built in 1851 as an improved version of the Iron Dukes, with 140 lb pressure instead of 100 lb. A comparison with *Sultan* will show that sanding gear has been fitted, the 'cab' has been improved by the addition of small side sheets and 'elephant ear' spectacles fitted on the backplate. The final form of Gooch chimney has been fitted, although this was probably a later addition. *Lord of the Isles* had an eventful career, being exhibited at the Great Exhibition of 1851, at Edinburgh in 1890, Earls Court in 1897, and Chicago in 1893. She also had the doubtful distinction of hauling the Directors' special for the opening of the line to Birmingham, on which duty she collided with another train at Aynho. She was withdrawn from service in 1884 after running approximately 789,000 miles with her original boiler. She was stored at Swindon until 1906, when unfortunately she was broken up together with *North Star*. Still she would not die, for her driving wheels turned up at the 1951 Festival of Britain and now rest in Swindon Museum.

Europa. One of Gooch's standard 5'0" goods engines, built at Swindon in 1853. She was the only one out of 102 which was rebuilt, with a new boiler and an Armstrong cab, in June 1869. This raises an interesting point, as the photograph is supposed to have been taken in June 1869, which is difficult to believe as surely no engine could deteriorate to this apparent condition within a month of rebuilding. *Europa* worked on the Wilts and Somerset line and was later transferred to Plymouth. She was alleged to have been the last broad gauge engine to leave Plymouth, in the early hours of Saturday, May 21st 1892.

Dewrance. One of the 'Hawthorn' class of 6′0″, 2–4–0s built by Slaughter, Gruning and Company of Bristol in 1865. This class of 26 engines was named after famous engineers; one was in fact named after the founder of the builders–*Slaughter*. Fortunately, the company changed its name to the Avonside Engine Company late in 1865 and *Slaughter* became *Avonside* before it had an opportunity to justify its name. These engines were originally used on the Wilts and Somerset line and *Dewrance* was transferred to the Plymouth area after 1876. Here it often hauled ocean mails trains to Bristol. Of interest is the non-standard tender and wooden extensions to the buffers. She remained in service until the final abolition of the broad gauge in 1892. One of the class, *Headley*, survived in stationary use until 1929.

Stewart. Another of the 'Hawthorn' class, but *Stewart*, together with nine others, was rebuilt in 1877 with 5'0" wheels and saddle tanks. They were used for service west of Exeter, where this particular engine worked until the end, in 1892.

Sir Watkin, one of six engines with 4′6″ wheels built in 1866 and known as the 'Sir Watkin' class. Designed by Armstrong as evidenced by the dome (which was unusual on pure broad gauge engines), and the typical Armstrong safety valve cover. Originally built as condensing side tanks for use on the Metropolitan Railway, they were soon made redundant on that line by its conversion to narrow gauge in 1869. Three engines were sold to the South Devon Railway where they were fitted with short saddle tanks in addition to the side tanks, as shown on page 45. The remaining three were altered to the condition shown in this photograph and those running on the South Devon line were modified to conform, after amalgamation in 1876.

Note the improvised side sheets and roof fitted to the original weatherboard, and the buffer extensions. *Sir Watkin* was withdrawn from service in 1892.

Antiquary, built in 1855 by Robert Stephenson and Co. Ltd. of Newcastle. There were nine others known as the 'Waverley' class and had 7′0″ coupled wheels. Shown here as built, with early pattern chimney and no spectacle plates, she makes a splendid sight with her polished brass running board edging shining in the summer sun. These engines were mainly based on Swindon, working to Gloucester, South Wales, and Bristol. *Antiquary* remained in service until 1876.

Bulkeley, one of what must have been the most well-known of all broad gauge classes, the 'Rovers'. These 26 engines were built at Swindon in small batches between 1871 and 1888 to replace the almost identical 'Iron Dukes' and 'Couriers' with the same names, which were reaching the end of their useful life. The broad gauge was doomed, it was not considered worthwhile to produce a new design of express locomotive, and the 'Iron Dukes' had been so successful in service that the new engines were built to the original design, but with a small increase in boiler pressure. They were all fitted with cabs, which improved the appearance and the enginemen's 'lot' considerably; compare the illustration of *Bulkeley's* cab interior with that of *Sultan*. The end views show the advantage given by the wider gauge, but also shows that the opportunity was never taken to increase the proportions of the engine accordingly.

A splendidly posed photograph of 'Rover' class engine *Crimea*. The date is given as September 1878, which is also shown as the building date, therefore one can assume that a proud shed foreman has assembled his staff around his new acquisition for the photographer to record for posterity. This engine replaced the 'Iron Duke' class engine of the same name which ran between 1855 and 1876. Note the gong on the tender, which was connected to the front van of the train by a cord and enabled the guard to 'communicate' with the driver.

A 'Rover' class 8 foot single *Sebastopol*, simmering in Newton Abbot yard on July 28th, 1890. This view shows the tender to advantage and illustrates the position of the re-railing jacks on the buffer beam. The tool boxes are in an unusual position, but are usefully employed in holding back those king-sized lumps of coal.

BRISTOL AND EXETER RAILWAY LOCOMOTIVES

No. 46, one of Pearson's first series of eight 4–2–4 well tanks. With their 9 foot driving wheels and tall, bell-mouthed chimney, they appeared to have more in common with paddle steamers than railway locomotives. They were employed on fast passenger services, and one was recorded at nearly 82 m.p.h. down the Wellington bank. With only brakes on the rear bogie one wonders if this high speed was intentional or whether the engine was running away. These fantastic machines had a relatively short life, being withdrawn between 1868 and 1873.

B. & E.R. No. 40, later became G.W.R. No. 2002. This was one of a class of 4 engines built between 1868 and 1873 as replacements for the original 9 foot 4–2–4 tanks and were basically similar, but with inside frames to all wheels and driving wheel diameter reduced to 8′10″. They were probably even more legendary than their predecessors and were surely no less startling in appearance. No. 40 originally had an all-over roof in one bent sheet forming weatherboard, roof, and backplate, but this was removed after the amalgamation presumably to conform with the Great Western *fresh air for enginemen* policy. Of interest in the photograph are the very large, and probably very necessary, sandboxes on the engine and the branch disc-and-crossbar signal in the background.

On the 27th July 1876, the up 'Flying Dutchman', hauled by 4–2–4 T No. 2001 was derailed at Long Ashton, and the driver and fireman were killed. No. 2001 was scrapped and the remaining three engines of the class were rebuilt in 1877 as 4–2–2 tender engines, as personified by No. 2002 above. The rebuilding, which included the reduction in driving wheel diameter to 8′0″, produced a far better proportioned machine, perhaps the best on the broad gauge. They continued in express work in conjunction with the 'Rover' class 4–2–2s, and were withdrawn in 1884, 1889, and 1890; the last to go being No. 2002.

No. 2017, built in 1871 as B. & E.R. No. 5 was one of the Pearson's first class of ten passenger tender engines. These had a reputation for being rough riders. The majority were shedded at Bristol and worked mainly to Newton Abbot. No. 2017 was based on Plymouth for a while, but was considered unsuitable for working the heavily graded lines in the district due to her large diameter driving wheels. However, she remained in service until 1892.

No. 2052, originally B. & E.R. No. 89, built by the Avonside Engine Company in 1873, was one of a class of twenty-six basically similar engines built by various builders between 1855 and 1873. With 5'6" coupled wheels, they were well-liked machines, being used on both main and branch lines. Upon conversion to the narrow gauge of the branches east of Exeter, they were moved further west and ended their careers mainly on the South Devon and Cornwall lines. A sister engine to 2052, No. 2051, was involved in the Norton Fitzwarren accident on November 11th, 1890. Whilst working an up Liner Special Express from Plymouth, she collided head-on with a down narrow gauge goods which had been reversed onto the up road to allow another train to pass, and had been forgotten. Ten passengers were killed and No. 2051 was damaged beyond repair. No. 2052 survived until 1892. Note the additions to the weatherboard to form a primitive cab, and the provision of screw reverse.

SOUTH DEVON RAILWAY LOCOMOTIVES

After the 'Atmospheric' fiasco, the South Devon Railway turned to Gooch to design powerful passenger locomotives capable of tackling 1 in 40 gradients and sharp curves, and he produced the unusual but practical 'Corsair' class 4—4—0 saddle tank in 1851. These were built, with various detail alterations, throughout the independent existence of the Company. In 1866, the Company took over locomotive working from the contractors, Messrs. Evans and Geach (later Evans, Walker and Gooch) who had been operating the line since 1851, and in that year bought a batch of six engines of the basic 'Corsair' type from the Avonside Engine Company, of which *Gorgon* is an example. She was photographed in November 1891 at Newton Abbot, with the abolition of the broad gauge and the end of her life only six months away.

The S.D.R. purchased further batches of 4–4–0 saddle tanks of different types, and two examples are illustrated here. No. 2134 *Heron*, with her sister *Magpie*, were built in 1861 by Sharp, Stewart and hired for service on the Carmarthen and Cardigan Railway until 1872. They were then purchased by the South Devon, who fitted them with saddle tanks. They were the most conventional of all the South Devon 4–4–0s and, for that reason, were the odd men out.

Leopard, No. 2128, was one of a pair of engines built by Avonside in 1872 designed for easy conversion to narrow gauge. They were, however, never converted and after withdrawal were employed shunting the broad gauge scrapyard at Swindon until June 1893, when they were cut up.

No. 2155, *Romulus*, was one of a pair of 4'9" goods engines built for the S.D.R. by Avonside in November, 1866, her sister engine being, understandably, *Remus*. This photograph is alleged to have been taken in 1876, by which time a primitive cab had been added to her weatherboard. *Romulus* lasted until 1892.

No. 2170, *Taurus*. This was a one-off machine, with 3′0″ wheels, built in 1869 by Avonside. She was employed on the Brixham, Sutton Harbour, and Ashburton branches and converted to narrow gauge in 1894. She was re-numbered 1326, and probably continued in the same duties as in her broad gauge days until her withdrawal in 1905. Note the distinctive cab and low running plate.

Owl, one of three 0–4–0 shunting tanks with 3′0″ wheels and well tanks built in 1873 by Avonside and designed to be convertible to narrow gauge. They were named *Owl*, *Weasel*, and *Goat*—incongruous nomenclature, but possibly more appropriate than the usual names taken at random from mythology. Upon amalgamation, these engines were numbered 2172 to 2174. *Weasel* was withdrawn to become a portable engine, and *Owl* and *Goat* were sold to contractors who used them in connection with the doubling of the main line to Plymouth. The Great Western bought them back in 1893, converted them to narrow gauge, fitted cabs and saddle tanks, and re-numbered them 1327 and 1328, in which guise they survived until 1913 and 1910 respectively. This photograph is credited to have been taken in 1876.

Raven, No. 2175, another 3'0" 0–4–0 tank with a chequered history. One of five built by Avonside in 1874 for use in the Plymouth Docks. She was sold to the Torbay and Brixham Railway in 1877 and taken into G.W. stock upon the absorption of that line in 1883. She was converted to narrow gauge in 1892, re-numbered 1329 and fitted with a new boiler. She was subsequently sold to the Wantage Tramway where she was said to be prone to derailment, and cut up at Wantage in 1920 after a period of inactivity. Note the spark arrester on the chimney and the buffer extensions.

CONVERTIBLE LOCOMOTIVES

By 1876 it was clear that the final abolition of the broad gauge was imminent and it was therefore decided not to produce new designs of locomotives. Apart from the 'Rovers', all replacement stock was to be convertible to narrow gauge and most of the engines built were narrow gauge designs temporarily fitted with extended axles, wheels, and frames. No. 1561 was such a machine. One of a batch of Armstrong's standard gauge '1134' class 0–6–0 saddle tanks modified for service on the broad gauge, with wheels surmounted by a typical broad gauge curved footplate. She was probably based on Newton Abbot and was re-converted in 1892. Some of these engines ran on passenger services with the rear coupling rods removed, as 0–4–2s.

No. 1205, one of Armstrong's '388' class, otherwise known as the 'Standard Goods'. She was built in 1876, one of the last batch of 20. She was converted to broad gauge in June 1876 and subsequently fitted with a cab. The combination of a tall, narrow cab with a wide tender from an old broad gauge engine gave her a decidedly odd appearance. This class was mainly used for through goods traffic between Plymouth and London, and they were re-converted during 1892.

No. 3509, one of a class of ten 2–4–0 tanks built with 5′1″ wheels in 1885 as broad gauge convertibles. Five of these were rebuilt as tender engines in 1890/91, but 3509 remained as a tank. The whole class was rebuilt as tender engines when converted in 1892 and assimilated into the '3201' or 'Stella' class.

No. 14 was one of a pair of 2–4–0s with 7'0½" wheels built in 1888 especially for working the heavy 3.00 p.m. express from Bristol to London. They were handsome machines, with typical Dean features, and the large driving wheels were complemented proportionally by the 4'6½" leading wheels. Nos. 14 and 16 were withdrawn in 1892 and the intention was to rebuild them as narrow gauge 2–4–0s similar in appearance to the 'Barnum' class, but after the decision to rebuild the 'Wigmore Castle' 2–2–2s with front bogies, two 4–4–0s appeared, numbered 14 and 16. There are conflicting views as to the amount of the original engines remaining in these 'rebuilds', some even say that only the numbers were re-used. In their subsequent careers they lost these as well, ending their days as 'Flower' class taper-boiler 4–4–0s numbered 4169 and 4170. This is surely a tale to rival that of the legendary Irishman's hammer, which with two new heads and three new handles was still as good as the day it was bought.

No. 3022. One of ten of Dean's narrow gauge 'Wigmore Castle' class to be temporarily fitted with broad gauge wheels and axles to assist with increased traffic during the last few months before the final gauge conversion in 1892. They were re-converted during 1892 and 3022 was named *Rougemont*, fitted with a leading bogie in 1894, and re-named *Bessemer* in 1898. In her latter days, as one of the famous 'Dean Singles', her appearance was a far cry from the gawky but purposeful machine illustrated here.

ALONG THE LINE

Acton station in mixed gauge days, probably in 1876 or 1877. This view was taken looking east, with the signals for the junction of the line to Willesden visible beyond the station building. Note the hand lever between the main lines, which appears to be a primitive form of locking device.

Maidenhead Bridge signal box, a typical box of the period, probably photographed in 1892. The hamper is rather intriguing. Did it contain important dispatches, or merely the signalman's lunch?

Bristol Temple Meads, said to have been photographed in 1875, showing the Bristol and Exeter train shed on the left, the Bristol and Exeter offices in the centre, and the Great Western station on the right. This picture has been published several times before, but the wealth of period details shown warrants its inclusion in this volume.

Wootton Bassett station in mixed gauge days, looking east towards Swindon. The van in the yard is of interest, as is the mixture of disc and crossbar and semaphore signals. The photographer must have had a very commanding personality, as he has captured the attention of everyone in the picture, even the shunting horse and the dog.

ENGINES AT REST

A South Devon Railway locomotive yard pictured some time between 1872 and 1876. Nearest the camera is 4–4–0 saddle tank *Heron*, in an earlier condition than that depicted on page 30. Behind *Heron* is one of the three 'Sir Watkin' class engines described on page 18 which were sold to the South Devon Railway in 1872.

A delightful scene at Newton Abbot by the Rev. A. H. Malan taken on July 17th, 1889. In the foreground is 'Hawthorn' class 2–4–0 *Wood* waiting to take over the train which has been brought in by the Armstrong saddle tank, now making its way to the shed. A 'Rover' class 8 foot single can be seen on the right hand track.

Ex-Bristol and Exeter Railway 4—2—2 No. 2001 at Dawlish in 1883. This sister engine to 2002, shown on page 26 was originally numbered 2005 as a 4—2—4 tank, but was re-numbered 2001 upon re-building to take the place of the engine scrapped after the Long Ashton accident, and to confuse twentieth century historians.

'Rover' class 8 foot singles *Rover* and *Iron Duke* photographed on November 11th, 1890 at Bristol by the Rev. A. H. Malan. The quality of the photograph and the sharpness of detail is remarkable, as is the pristine condition of the engines. Even the cab floor on *Iron Duke* looks clean enough to eat off.

ACCIDENTS

A superb trio of photographs showing clearing-up operations after the Bullo Pill accident of November 5th, 1868. At that time the South Wales line was operated by the 'ten minute' method of signalling, by which the signals at stations were kept at danger for ten minutes after the departure of a train, and then cleared until such time as a further train passed. The idea being that a minimum ten minute headway would prevent rear end collisions. However, on this occasion, this primitive method was no safeguard. An up cattle train from Carmarthen stuck in the section, and the 5.00 p.m. mail from New Milford, running past clear signals at about ten o'clock at night, ran straight into the rear of the cattle train. Reports differ, but between three and eight men in the rear van died, and about thirty-six beasts were either killed in the collision or had to be destroyed afterwards. In view of the force of impact, the condition of *Rob Roy* is remarkably good, and after repair she continued in traffic until 1872. The careful posing of the personnel is typical of the period, and the thatched permanent way hut is worthy of study.

This photograph had to be included—if only for the caption: 'an exploded view of a Gooch 8 foot single'. The boiler of *Perseus* exploded at Westbourne Park shed on November 8th, 1862 and, impossible as it may seem from this picture, it was rebuilt and ran until December 1880. Surely a tribute to Gooch's sandwich frame construction and contemporary workmanship.

The first broad gauge train at Redruth, in 1866. Note the extremely low roofed carriage, exaggerated by the height of the chimney on *Lance*, which was one of the first South Devon engines referred to on page 29. *Lance* was built in 1851 and scrapped in 1873 as a result of damage received in the farcical Menheniot collision. In this, two goods trains were standing at Menheniot awaiting the road, and the signal porter, having obtained 'line clear' for the down train, called out 'Right away, Dick' to the guard. The guard of the *up* train, unfortunately also called Dick, promptly started his double-headed train, which met another down goods halfway to St. Germans. All three engines were damaged, and *Lance*, to quote MacDermot, being '*quite destroyed*'.

Marazion station in 1867, showing a goods train hauled by South Devon engine *Dido,* which was built in 1860 and withdrawn in 1877 as Great Western No. 2143. The goods traffic on the West Cornwall line at that time warranted but one through goods train per day, which was broad gauge until 1871, after which it was operated as a 'mixed' train, with narrow gauge wagons in front followed by a match truck and the rake of broad gauge wagons. The mind boggles at the thought of this ensemble negotiating mixed gauge pointwork.

A charming shot of a 'Rover' class 8 foot single in the latter years of the broad gauge, with a down main line train composed of Dean narrow bodied bogie stock. The conventional narrow gauge track contrasts sharply with the broad gauge 'baulk road'.

The following few photographs, and several others in this collection, were taken by the Rev. A. H. Malan, who lived at Teignmouth in the 1880s, and evidently knew the right way to obtain a track pass. When one considers the bulky, crude cameras and slow speeds of the period, his pictures must be acknowledged as being amongst the best examples of his time. Apart from technical merit, the outstanding features of all of his photographs are action and pictorial composition. They all give a graphic impression of a particular scene brought to life by the motion of the train or the actions of the railwaymen; all framed in an impeccably chosen background which would do credit to many of today's experts.

In the twilight of the broad gauge, when he was resident in Shropshire, he returned to his old haunts to make a further photographic record, this time of the end of an era.

His collection is in the possession of the British Railways Board Archivist, a fitting resting place for a treasured record of the last years of the broad gauge.

A 'Rover' class hauled express thrashes its way through the rain at Stoke Canon in May 1891.

A very well-known picture taken at Teignmouth, again in May 1891, with 'Rover' class *Timour* accelerating away with an up express.

The 'North Mail', photographed near Exminster on May 5th, 1891, drawn by 'Rover' class 8 foot single *Warlock*. Of interest is the cross-sleepered track, very rare on the broad gauge; the distant signal with vertical white band, and the motley collection of rolling stock.

An almost unbelievably immaculate 'Rover' class engine, *Amazon*, stands at Newton Abbot on July 25th, 1883, accompanied by a quartet of hard-hatted admirers. The width of the old broad coaching stock can be judged by the low-roofed, oil lit, six wheeler behind the tender.

An express, hauled by the usual 'Rover' class engine, storming along the straight and level main line near Brent Knoll in May, 1891.

The down 'Cornishman' passing Uphill Junction behind 'Rover' class *Emperor* in the charge of driver Gorwill. A narrow gauge goods train is waiting on the down line from Weston-super-Mare, which is not laid with the third rail. The down main line refuge is also only laid for narrow gauge trains.

A fine action shot of the mails being picked up at Cullompton in May 1891, with the postman anxiously watching the transfer.

The down 'Flying Dutchman' passing Weston Junction with driver George Eggar saluting. The signalman seems more intent on the camera than the driver's acknowledgment.

A photograph which I have chosen for its composition, but about which I know nothing. The train, headed by the inevitable 'Rover', is presumably one of the principal down expresses, to judge from its formation. The location seems to be vaguely familiar, and I would hazard a guess at West Drayton. Note the branch train simmering in the background.

'Rover' class *Dragon* pauses for the camera whilst the station staff scowl at the photographer. The enthusiasts are too interested in the innards of *Dragon* to realise that their images are being recorded for posterity.

The down 'Flying Dutchman' passing Twyford on May 14th, 1892, drawn by 'Rover' class *Eupatoria*. Of interest are the different connections to the siding for broad and narrow gauge, and the bridge in the process of being rebuilt in connection with the quadrupling of the line.

Another down Cornish express also at Twyford on the same day, but this time hauled by a Dean 2–2–2 Convertible No. 3027. This engine had less than a week left running in its broad gauge state. It is interesting to learn that our Victorian ancestors had learnt the art of leaning on brooms.

The last broad gauge 'Cornishman', 10.15 a.m. from Paddington on Friday, May 20th, 1892, headed by *Great Western*, pauses for the camera before making its historic journey. Among the top-hatted gentry are George Armstrong, Wolverhampton Locomotive Superintendent, in front of the centre of the tender; and to his left, Joseph Armstrong's son John, who was at the time London Divison Locomotive Superintendent.

The same train, later on the same day, and now headed by *Dragon*, pauses for water at Taunton and attracts the usual crowd, including the local Permanent Way gang who are about to experience the most hectic weekend of their lives.

One of the many 'last up broad gauge trains' on Friday, May 20th, 1892. The engine is alleged to be *Bulkeley*, but she is also supposed to have brought up the *very* last train, which arrived at Paddington at 5.30 a.m. on the 21st. The location, however, cannot be questioned. It is Sonning Cutting, a view of which no book on the Great Western should be without.

GAUGE CONVERSION

A gauge conversion gang with a special train at Grange Court during the narrowing of the Gloucester and Hereford line in August 1869. This photograph, although it is well-known, had to be included to illustrate the size of the operation and the manpower needed, as well as the lengths some people would go to in order to get into the limelight. How those worthies got to the top of the signals we can only wonder, and goodness knows how long they had to hold their poses.

Gauge conversion work at Plymouth Millbay in May 1892. The new pointwork had been fabricated previously, which is why, in this view, the old crossings are being removed piecemeal.

THE BROAD GAUGE MORTUARY

The broad gauge 'dump' at Swindon in 1892. Apart from the 'convertibles', which were rapidly altered, there were only 60 pure broad gauge engines in existence at the end, including the 23 surviving 'Rovers', a line of which stand forlornly on the nearest track. These were gradually broken up during 1892 and the first few months of 1893.

These two photographs were taken at the same time from adjacent positions. The bunker of No. 3553, on the right hand side on page 74, is that shown in the foreground on page 75. The first two rows on page 74, reading from left to right, are mainly South Devon tanks, interspersed with a few convertibles; row 3 are all convertibles, mainly 'Standard Goods'; row 4 are mainly convertible 0–6–0 saddle tanks with a few South Devon 4–4–0 tanks; row 5 are again 0–6–0 convertibles, both tender and tank; row 6 are 'Rovers'; row 7 contains several 0–4–4T convertibles; and row 8 and 9 are again 'Rovers'.

On page 75, rows 8 and 9 are shown in close up, and one can see to advantage the cleanliness of the stock—a far cry from the scene at the end of standard gauge steam.

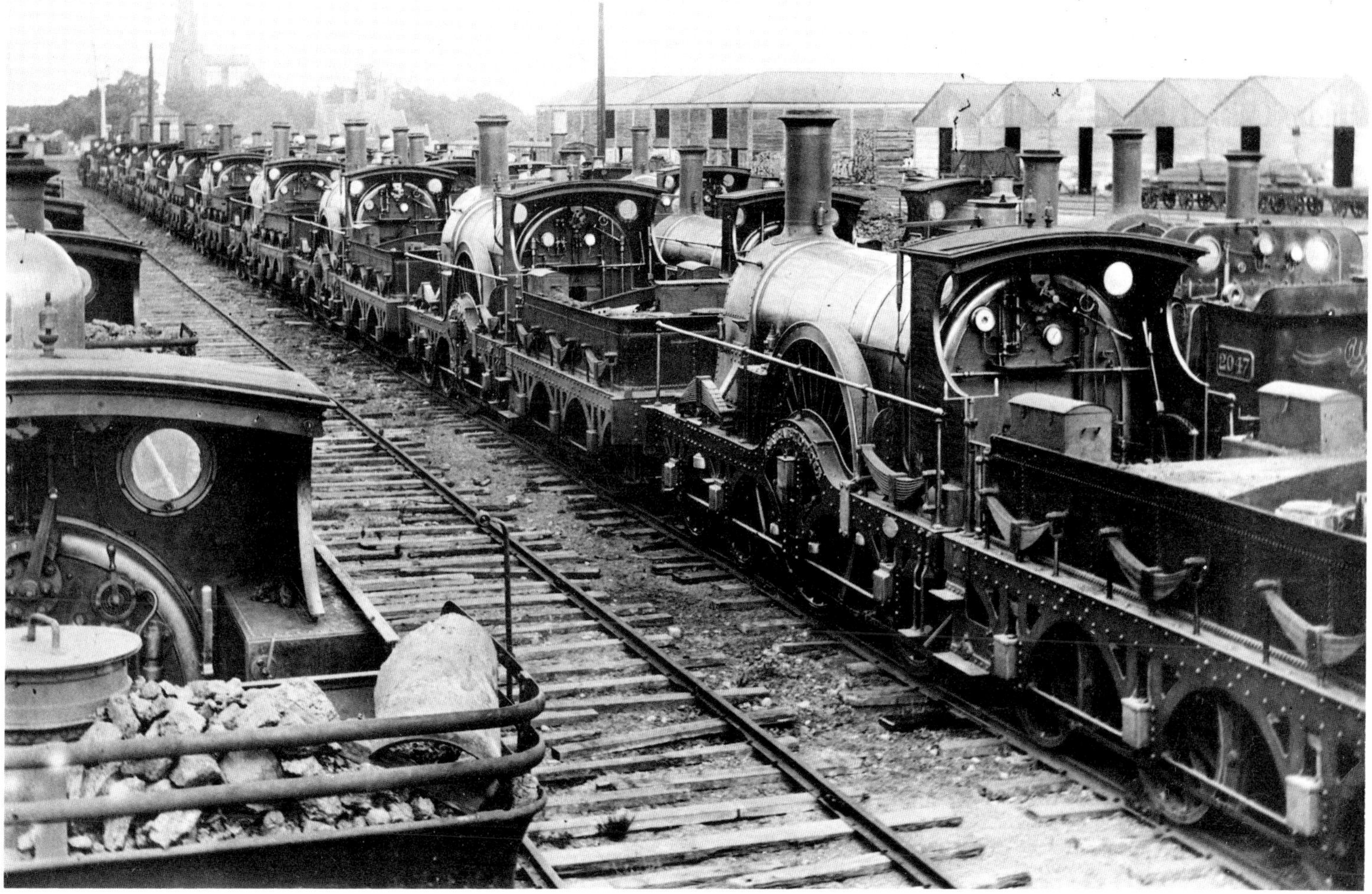
2047

This photograph was taken from the other side of the 'dump', from approximately the spot where the gentleman is surveying the scene on page 73. In the foreground are ex South Devon 0–6–0ST *Argo* and *Hawthorn* class 2–4–0ST *Roberts*.

Broad gauge coaching stock in the stockyard at Swindon in 1892. The convertible stock is apparent from the wide footboards.

Broad gauge freight stock awaiting cutting up at Swindon in 1892.

The last photograph, and the only narrow or standard gauge one in this book. It depicts an inspection train at Whiteball, presumably in the process of checking the line after conversion, and is thus a fitting note on which to end.

THE BURIAL OF THE 'BROAD-GAUGE.'

Not a whistle was heard, not a brass bell-note,
As his course o'er the sleepers we hurried;
Not a fog-signal wailed from a husky throat
O'er the grave where our 'Broad-Gauge' we buried.

We buried him darkly, at dead of night,
The sod with our pickaxes turning,
By the danger-signal's ruddy light,
And our oil-lamps dimly burning.

No useless tears, though we loved him well!
Long years to his fire-box had bound us.
We fancied we glimpsed the great shade of BRUNEL
In sad sympathy hovering round us.

Few and gruff were the words we said,
But we thought, with a natural sorrow,
Of the Narrow-Gauge foe of the Loco. just dead,
We should have to attend on the morrow.

We thought, as we hollowed his big broad bed,
And piled the brown earth o'er his funnel,
How his foe o'er the Great-Western metals would tread,
Shrieking triumph through cutting and tunnel.

Lightly they'll talk of him now he is gone,
For the cheap 'Narrow Gauge' has outstayed him,
Yet BULL *might* have found, had he let it go on,
That BRUNEL's Big Idea would have paid him!

But the battle is ended, our task is done;
After forty years' fight he's retiring.*
This hour sees thy Triumph, O STEPHENSON;
Old 'Broad Gauge' no more will need firing.

The 'Dutchman' must now be 'divided in two'!—
Well, well, they shan't mangle or mess *you*!
Accept the last words of friends faithful, if few:—
'Good-bye, poor old Broad-Gauge, God bless you!'†

Slowly and sadly we laid him down,
He has filled a great chapter in story.
We sang not a dirge—we raised not a stone,
But we left the 'Broad Gauge' to his glory!